*C*ities literally transform the earth, turn farms into parking lots and waste enormous amounts of time and energy transporting people, goods and services over their expanses. *The alternative is urban implosion rather than explosion. In nature, as an organism evolves, it increases in complexity and it also becomes a more compact or miniaturized system. A city should function similarly in order to support the complex activities that sustain human culture. Cities are the necessary instrument for the evolution of humankind.*

Paolo Soleri

ARCOSANTI ARCHETYPE

The Rebirth of Cities
by Renaissance Thinker Paolo Soleri

●

by
Marie Wilson

**Photography
by
Michel Sarda**

Freedom Editions
Fountain Hills, Arizona

Acknowledgements

A special thanks to Jackie Engel and Lori Carroll, Public Relations Department, Cosanti Foundation, for their help in coordinating my efforts to complete *Arcosanti Archetype*. Heartfelt thanks to Kathleen Evans, Fountain Hills, Arizona, who put so much effort into editing my manuscript. The advice and support of Marsha and Robert Falco has been invaluable.

Published by Freedom Editions
16817B East Hawk Drive
Fountain Hills AZ 85268
Phone (480) 836-8704 • Fax (480) 836-8704
E-mail: mwilson @ inficad.com

Book design: Sarda Resources, Inc., Phoenix

Library of Congress Card Number: 98-96938
ISBN 0-9668086-0-6

Printed by Gilliland Printing, Arkansas City, KS

TABLE OF CONTENTS

Comments from the Photographer

Training as an architect in Paris, France, I discovered Paolo Soleri's work in the early 1960s, when many considered his projects "architecture-fiction." Many still do. I was first attracted by the sheer magnitude of these extraordinary designs, where human beings become a part of something larger than anything they have conceived before.

Today, the exponential growth of the world population, the emergence of an immense consumers' market in Asia and the urban explosion (the Tokyo and Mexico City metropolitan areas each have a population of more than 25 million, larger than all of Canada) are bringing the Arcology concept into a new perspective. We are becoming aware that the uncontrolled destruction of our environment leads to global disaster. Radical new solutions must be considered to keep our planet liveable for an ever-increasing population. With the spirit and faith of a pioneer, Paolo Soleri started exploring these solutions fifty years ago. Arizona's magnificent scenery certainly contributed to this faith and spirit.

Soleri's work goes far beyond the pressing necessity to salvage our environment and to offer decent housing to humankind. Soleri inscribes this necessity into a much larger scope, that is, the largest there is – the evolution of the universe from its origin to its end.

It was my privilege to meet with this outstanding figure of our time and to cooperate with him and his staff on a variety of initiatives. I am grateful to Marie Wilson for giving me an opportunity to pay personal homage to Paolo Soleri with the photography that I contributed to this book.

Michel Sarda

Introduction

A few years ago I read a magazine article about Paolo Soleri, Ph.D. and Arcosanti. Intrigued with his innovative ideas, I thought about visiting Arcosanti, a work in progress, and meeting the man whose extraordinary vision could be influential in training new generations to conserve resources, minimize adverse impacts on the environment and, in the process, elevate humanity to a higher level of consciousness.

Three years later, while driving from Phoenix with a friend to visit the Grand Canyon, I was reminded of Soleri when I saw a sign pointing to Arcosanti. I asked my friend to take the winding dirt road. We soon found the oasis in the desert known as Arcosanti.

We embarked on a tour during which an enthusiastic guide presented an overview of Paolo Soleri's philosophy. I then studied Soleri's drawings of his futuristic cities designed to reduce the size of cities thereby minimizing urban sprawl and the impact on the environment. I thought, "Perhaps in our lifetime, we will not have cities as Soleri envisions, but I believe the influence of his work will be realized in generations to come."

I believe we have an opportunity to examine the problems connected with urban sprawl, inspiring in each of us new thoughts and new aspirations that will give new meaning to life. Perhaps my efforts will provoke thoughts among the readers that will serve as an impetus to incorporate the concepts of Dr. Soleri and make changes for the betterment of humanity. At Arcosanti the perfect opportunity exists to experiment, gain knowledge and merge the beneficial ideas into our lives. Together we can be the catalysts to bring about changes idealized by Paolo Soleri to protect the environment and minimize the impact of our increasing population through political, social and economic reforms. Arcosanti's focus is to help find answers to critical questions. With habitat loss, ozone depletion, pollution and emerging social issues, the crisis is real and action is necessary now.

Although much has been written about Paolo Soleri and his ideas, his philosophy has yet to be incorporated into the concepts of modern urban planners. Soleri's persistent refusal to follow the established route and his struggle toward a more meaningful life for people together with his emphasis on the preservation of the environment, as in Soleri's words, will help, "to redevelop a culture that might not be so imprisoned by its own needs."

(continued)

My contribution, through this book, is to urge readers to discover the trailblazing ideas of Paolo Soleri represented by the archetypal town of Arcosanti. Together we can discover how Soleri's miniaturized cities can offer a more cohesive environment where people can eliminate wasteful travel time in massive traffic jams, reduce urban sprawl and its detrimental effects and have the added benefit of more leisure time to enjoy cultural activities and the natural habitat surrounding their city.

All of this underscores my ongoing concern for our environment. Our diverse land is too precious to destroy through endless urban sprawl. I believe we have an obligation to preserve the environment for generations to come. It is my deepest hope that readers will not only read the story of Paolo Soleri and Arcosanti but also share it with family, friends and community leaders.

Marie Wilson

The problem I am confronting is the present design of cities only a few stories high, stretching outward in unwieldy sprawl for miles. As a result of their sprawl, they literally transform the earth, turn farms into parking lots and waste enormous amounts of time and energy transporting people, goods and services over their expanses. My solution is urban implosion rather than explosion. In nature, as an organism evolves, it increases in complexity, and it also becomes a more compact or miniaturized system. The city too is an organism of sorts—one that should be as alive and functional as any living creature. It must follow the same process of complexification and miniaturization to become a more lively container for the social, cultural and spiritual evolution of humankind.

The central concept around which these developments revolve is that of arcology — architecture and ecology as one integral process. Arcology is capable, at least theoretically, of demonstrating positive response to the many problems of urban civilization, those of population, pollution, energy and natural resource depletion, food scarcity and quality of life. Arcology is the methodology that recognizes the necessity of the radical reorganization of the sprawling urban landscape into dense integrated, three-dimensional cities. The city structure must contract, or miniaturize, in order to support the complex activities that sustain human culture and give it new perception and renewed trust in society and its future.

A central tenet of arcology is that the city is the necessary instrument for the evolution of humankind.

Paolo Soleri

Paolo Soleri, June 1998

The man is intensely focused. Paolo Soleri's life has been dedicated with great enthusiasm to his idealistic goals allowing little room for compromise.

He regrets society's indifference. "Society didn't make use of me. Part of that is my fault, I'm sure," Soleri remarks, "but it was too bad because if I had the resources, let's say, I could have done things that would have been far more impacting."

Background about Paolo Soleri

Leonardo da Vinci lived in exciting times – a time when faith and tradition gave way to learning and curiosity. This transitional movement, referred to historically as the Renaissance, began in the 14th Century and marked the division between medieval and modern times. The period was characterized by a humanistic revival of classical influence expressed in a flowering of the arts and literature and by the beginnings of modern science. Of all of this, da Vinci, a Florentine, was very much a part. It was an age of great accomplishments when a new kind of art was born.

Today, more than 500 years later, we have another Italian in our midst whose thinking will spark a modern Renaissance in how we think about our lives, our cities. Soleri's arcologies invite a sense of community where nature, architecture and the spiritual essence are as one. They encompass all aspects of life, including cultural, residential and commercial. The goal of arcology is to produce substantial buildings while addressing the needs of a growing world population. Emphasis is placed on the preservation of the environment.

To Soleri the impact of cities is the most critical issue of our time. He challenges us not only to examine the detrimental effect that urban sprawl has on the environment but to take action to contain this growth. He emphasizes that modern cities separate people from the natural world creating social isolation and ecological destruction. His ideas call for both a social and cultural revolution.

Soleri believes that suburbs promote segregation. He says, "Segregation is the most pervasive threat to the dignity and well-being of the individual and the group. There is an inherent logic in the structure and nature of organisms that have grown on this planet. Any architecture, any urban design, and any social order that violates that structure and nature is destructive of itself and of us. Any architecture, urban design, or social order that is based upon organic principles is valid and will prove its own validity. Land conservation will succeed only if and when man creates beautiful cities wherein he will feel it a privilege to be, live and work."

For both da Vinci and Soleri, nature gave rise to ideas that later found form. Da Vinci explored the countryside at a young age beginning his lifelong fascination with nature. During his early years Soleri hiked the Italian Alps with his father. Soleri recalls, "We didn't talk for hours. We walked and climbed. It was very physical. I realized years later, it was a great, great experience."

Soleri spent hundreds of hours wandering through the landscape, exploring the world of plants, trees and animals. Here he developed his insight about the connection between all organisms that would be the genesis for his ideas about architecture and the environment. This early connection to nature also prompted his study of religious concepts. He later would develop his own theories which he writes about in his publication, *The Omega Seed*, an enigmatic spiritual philosophy.

(continued)

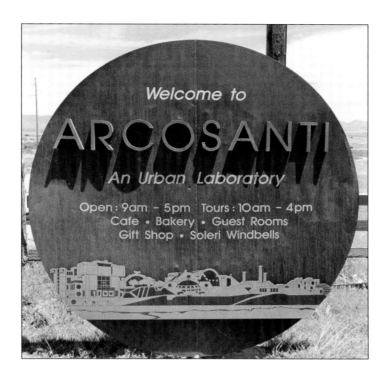

Soleri's talents gained him admittance for study at the Torino Polytechnic Institute in Turin, Italy, where he graduated with highest honors in his architectural studies and received his Ph.D. in architecture. Later, he received a scholarship and apprenticeship at Taliesin West with Frank Lloyd Wright; however, Soleri's path differed radically from that of Frank Lloyd Wright's mission for compatibility of the building with the environment. Soleri moved beyond Wright's mission of single buildings and environmental compatibility. He dealt with the clustering of the dwelling, the social effects of housing, the environmental impact of urban settings. Soleri added a global dimension with his ecological concerns to minimize growth.

These were busy and challenging years for Soleri. With this apprenticeship, Arizona became the youthful Soleri's playground in 1947. Here at Taliesin West he camped and collaborated with Mark Mills. Together they designed and constructed a glass-domed house (now called the Dome House) in Cave Creek. Their work was recognized for the unique heating and cooling system incorporated in the design.

For Soleri, the project offered an added benefit. He met and ultimately married Colly, the daughter of the family for whom the house was designed. Colly and Paolo enjoyed a harmonious relationship, raised two children and had two grandchildren. The marriage, however, was cut short by Colly's early death some years ago.

(continued)

Soleri filled thousands of pages with sketches of his cities of the future. A forward thinker of his time, Soleri developed plans for cities in outer space, on the ocean and even suspended over a canyon on top of a bridge. The seeds for Arcosanti were planted although it would be many years before construction would begin on his concept of a better future for humanity, which, Soleri believes, is a mere glimpse of what tomorrow's cities could and should be.

After Soleri's stint in the desert, he returned to Italy where he continued his studies and wrote about Cosmic Potentials. His research investigated the relationship of sun energy expressed in wind, infrared, hydrologic power and tidal changes to human habitats.

Soleri was commissioned to design a large ceramics factory in southern Italy. His experience with ceramics crafts led him to the production of cast clay and later to the manufacture of bronze windbells. These windbells would ultimately become the backbone of financing for the grander Arcosanti project.

In the fifties, Soleri returned to Arizona. With limited funding, Soleri established with his wife the non-profit Cosanti Foundation in Scottsdale that would serve as the springboard for the development of his humanistic ideas. His experimental earth house was developed on that land. Here he set up a foundry where visitors can purchase the now famous Arcosanti bells.

Ground was broken at Arcosanti in 1970. The vision was to build a prototype town with a contained population of up to 6,000. Soleri coined the term Arcology to represent his tenets, that is, architecture coherent with the ecology of the land. Within this context, scaled down cities would be built – he refers to this as miniaturization. Conversely, while minimizing the use of energy, raw materials and land which would effectively reduce waste and environmental pollution, the natural environment would surround the city.

The early phase of the project was to blend the architectural structures with the environment in a harmonious way. Although in the ensuing years, Arcosanti never reached its goal, it has served the purpose of embodying Soleri's unique blend of ideas for the city of the future. Arcosanti has provided Soleri with the opportunity to apply some of the concepts that he passionately believes are basic and fundamental. Here he says he can "test them to see if they work the way I think they ought to work. To leave something for posterity."

Since its inception, more than 50,000 people annually have passed across the dirt road and many have lived and participated in the on-going building of the structures. Others come for the annual dinner and concert series which started in 1980 and continues in memory of Colly Soleri.

Although often compared to da Vinci as a visionary, Soleri says, "It's boring to be too early." Soleri's dream is that Arcosanti will spark a renaissance in city planning before it's too late.

I am not designing cities. I am putting down ideas that are somehow opening a different perspective of what the city is involved in or could become. The question is not to demolish what exists but to guide how we add to that which exists in ways that may be conducive finally to a new form more responsive to the needs of society and to the needs of the environment.

I was lying in the sun and a fundamental aspect of what reality is came to me. There is a total connection between the domain of miniaturization and the domain of complexity and the two of them are really how the technology is developing that will bring a revolution.

Paolo Soleri

Paolo Soleri's Project

Ground was broken in June of 1970. For Soleri the notion of a town that would benefit humanity would, in fact, become reality. Although the growth of Arcosanti has been slow, the ongoing work serves as an archetype for future planning. Here ideas are being tested.

Soleri's inspiration was to build a town encompassing housing for up to 6,000 people on a small portion of the 860 acre desert site situated 65 miles north of Phoenix where buildings and the natural environment would co-exist. Here he would promote a style of living that would eliminate urban sprawl and its destructive forces. Since people would live, work, shop and experience their leisure time within easy walking distance, traffic jams would be a thing of the past. Automobiles would be reserved for trips outside the town limits. Arcosanti would be built upward to maximize space without sacrificing privacy. The tight clustering of buildings and services would allow for large parcels of natural acreage to be retained and set aside for agriculture and recreation.

Arcosanti is an experimental project inviting people of all ages to come together in a community. Some come to share in hands-on experiences of building and crafting and learning in daily or weekly workshop settings. Others come from all over the country to actually live in somewhat frugal conditions, learn a variety of skills and glean the wisdom of Soleri.

Groundbreaking was a moment of achievement for the Arcosantians in the early seventies.

"*We started doing the campsite so it was a temporary facility. It didn't have the flavor of a cornerstone. Then when we started the building on the site, people had a little sentiment about the building.*"

Paolo Soleri

The Arcosanti thinking of Paolo Soleri is represented in this scale model which is available for viewing in the Visitors' Gallery.

17

Visitors' Center
Includes Gallery,
Bakery, Café

Clay Bells
Apse

Residents' Housing

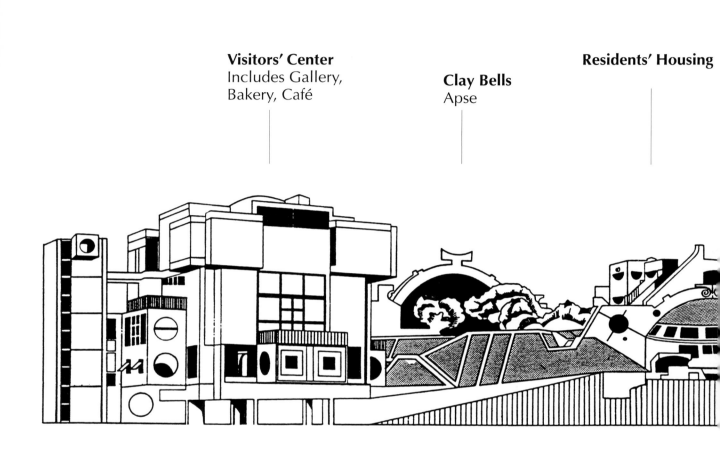

Staff Housing

Bronze Bell Foundr

Vaults   **Residents' Housing**   **Guest Housing**   **Office**

Colly Soleri Music Center

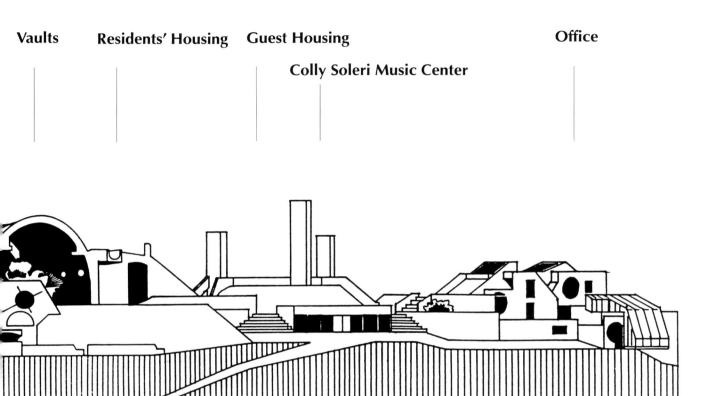

Library
Archives

Arcosanti Layout

The initial phase of Arcosanti, referred to as Old Town, consists of living quarters for about 100 residents. Apses (a design representing a quarter of a sphere) were built to house a bronze foundry and facility for ceramics where visitors can view the pouring and manufacturing of the now famous Arcosanti bells. The complex houses many studios where residents and volunteers can study, read, relax or socialize with one another.

The miniaturization of the city, that is, reduction in size and sprawl, in itself reduces the use of fossil fuels and the resultant pollution. Reliance on the automobile inside the city would be eliminated too thereby causing a huge reduction in fuel use. The buildings are carefully designed to maximize the sun for heat and shade for cooler temperatures, with angles and arches allowing for breezes and windows catching the natural light. Soleri believes that people thrive in environments that allow for natural lighting and natural views of the environment.

The apse in the ceramics and foundry areas is particularly interesting since it presents both Soleri's earth casting and solar energy concepts. The shell was poured in place using concrete over pre-shaped mounds of silt in a process where the earth is used as the mold to create a building. The earth-cast was then hollowed out or excavated. Soleri states, in his Earth Casting book, that "I have used this form because it can be applied in the context of a passive solar energy concept which I call the Apse Effect."

The Residents

Tomiaki Tamura, who comes from Kiryu near Tokyo, was intrigued with Soleri's futuristic city and the ideology of organic architecture. "I came to meet Paolo at Cosanti and then decided to do a six-week workshop but I stayed for 18 months."

Tomiaki began working part-time at Cosanti with Paolo while attending graduate school at Arizona State University. In 1983, he was invited to coordinate the project at Arcosanti. "I thought the project intent was very noble with a lot of potential to be explored. Although the construction is slow, we can encapsulate some essence of the project. A consumer-based society is very short sighted. We need to take a step back and look at where we are and see where we are heading. We can do something... a contribution to make change."

About his mentor, Paolo Soleri, Tamura says: "Soleri is shy and humble. Due to his uncompromising insistence he feels an important coherence with what is happening around us which gives him the energy to proceed. He is very consistent and I admire him for his commitment to what he believes."

David Tollas, who serves as Arcosanti's Construction Manager, thinks of Soleri's project as a seed. About his 11-year involvement, he says, "I am making a contribution to solve problems relating to energy, pollution and situations that don't cause urban sprawl. In that sense we have a common belief system working together. Paolo doesn't make compromises; he doesn't sell out, so it's slow. But gradually people are coming around."

Nadia Bégin and David are raising their 15-month-old son, Tristan, at Arcosanti. "Living here is intense. You have to do a transition, thinking in terms of less space and having respect for everybody else," says Nadia, who, in addition to her role as mother, is in charge of the architecture planning department. David adds, "You get into the philosophy of architecture, people's values, concept changes, sharing, morals, how to deal with people. It's a place to learn how this type of living might work."

"We feel lucky to be here," Nadia continues. "It is great to have our child with us all the time. Both of us can spend a lot of time with him. Everyone treats him like he is their child."

David and Nadia's main project is building additional spaces to house residents. Additional business and commercial spaces are also on the planning board.

As to working with Paolo, David says, "A nice collaboration comes to mind. He knows exactly how things should be within his style. You learn from that. He expects your opinion which he respects and considers. He depends on your talent."

Nadia thinks of her relationship with Paolo as one of apprentice to master. "My relationship with Paolo is more geared that way. We are really working for his ideas."

Some staff members, such as Tomiaki Tamura and Mary Hoadley, have been with the project since its inception. Soleri says warmly, "There is a continuity and dedication and luck on my part to have those people."

Mary Hoadley, who is known as the soul of Arcosanti, has been with the project since the start. She arrived at Arcosanti before ground was broken after casting off her 60's California lifestyle. Her daughter Katherine, now 14, is the first second generation Arcosantian. Hoadley thought Arcosanti made so much sense in all aspects, from the saving of resources to the absence of age segregation.

The sense of coherence and being part of the potential solution triggered in Hoadley the desire to stay. Here the concept includes both the urban and the wild. Living and working in close proximity to both allows for many options. She feels raising a child at Arcosanti has been full of added benefits. "It allowed me to stay with my daughter full time and still be part of everything with others helping out."

Hoadley's husband, Roger Tomalty, is the Primary Instructor for the Arcosanti workshop programs while Mary is the Site Coordinator.

The Foundry and Arcosanti Windbells

Foundry Manager, Steve Morse, an Arcosanti resident for several years, decided to become a permanent resident after serving as an apprentice in the foundry in 1990. Morse says one of the main benefits of living and working at Arcosanti is "being able to get up in the morning, get dressed and come to work. I don't like to commute." He also likes the exposure to a lot of people who spend time at Arcosanti, either long or short term.

On the early morning tour, visitors can observe the pouring of hot molten bronze to form the popular Arcosanti windbells. The sale of the bells helps to finance the on-going workshops, the building of Arcosanti and the payroll of more than 60 people. (Note: A foundry is also set up and bells can be purchased at the Cosanti Foundation Gallery in Scottsdale.)

The silicone bronze, which is popular with sculptors because it flows easily, is purchased by the ton and divided into ingots each weighing 16 to 20 pounds. The ingots are delivered on a pallet and then carried by a human chain from the loading zone up to the foundry where the ingots are stored.

The ingots are placed in a silicone carbide crucible which is then positioned in drums that are heated in the furnace up to 2600 degrees Fahrenheit. The bronze takes about an hour and a half to melt. Two people using a shank or hinged fork grippers then lift the crucible out. The foundry staff wears face shields and leather clothing to protect against burns. Leather burns slower and, in case of spattering hot bronze, allows time to remove clothing. "The clothing is hot and uncomfortable," says Morse who has had a couple of burns, "but it's better than being on fire."

The hot bronze is then poured into the Soleri designed sand molds. After the bronze has cooled, the sand is removed, the bells are cleaned and dipped into an acid bath of muriatic acid which accelerates oxidation. The bells take on a colorful green or maroon patina; however, the colors will continue to change after many years of exposure to the environment. Morse explains, "This process of oxidation takes about 30 minutes to accomplish what it would take nature 50 years to do."

Each bell has a different tone based on the size and weight – the bells can weigh as little as 4 or 5 pounds while Soleri's special assembly bells can be as heavy as 300 or 400 pounds. The large bells ring with a deeper lasting tone while smaller bells achieve a lighter, higher pitched tone.

The ceramic windbells are made from indigenous clay. The mixture of clay and water yields a material referred to as slip – a thick clay soup. Soleri originally developed the technique for slip casting earth bells by digging holes in the desert and casting the slip. Bells are cast from molds; freeform bells, from silt molds and spherical bells, from conventional plaster molds. Designs are hand carved into the damp surface before the bells are fired in a 2000 degrees Fahrenheit kiln.

Soleri's foundry is world famous. The Arcosanti bells are owned by many well-known personalities including Hugh Downs, Barbara Bush, Leo Buscaglia, James Garner. Even the Pope owns an Arcosanti bell.

(top left) Bronze ingots of up to 20 pounds are heated in a 2600° Fahrenheit furnace.

(top right) Removal of the crucible holding the melted bronze.

(above left) Bronze is poured into sand-filled molds.

(above right) The bells, after being dipped in an acid bath which gives them a colorful patina, are hung in the apse that houses the foundry.

Creative and colorful, Arcosanti bells are ideal for adding warmth and music to indoor or outdoor settings. The designs often incorporate elements of nature such as dolphins and birds. There is a line of special assemblies. In these various pieces fit together allowing for movement along with the musical sound of the bell itself. These Soleri bells are sculpted by the master himself.

Paolo Soleri was honored in 1963 with the American Institute of Architects Gold Medal of Craftsmanship for his creative bell designs.

In order to encourage creative endeavors, Paolo Soleri designed the Arizona "Support The Arts" bell.

Cause Bells

Soleri's Cause Bells are designed to depict an issue of either national or global concern. Each time a Cause Bell is purchased, $16.00 is given directly to one of the stated organizations according to the request of the buyer. Since the inception of the project in 1985, organizations such as The Nature Conservancy of Arizona, the AIDS Foundation and Friends of the River have benefited with a portion of the more than $275,000 raised through the sale of Cause Bells.

Some of the organizations
to whom donations flow:
AIDS Foundation
Arizona Diabetes Association
Arizona Opera League
Audubon Society
Desert Botanical Gardens
Friends of the River
Humane Society of Arizona
Make a Wish Foundation
Monterey Bay Aquarium
Nature Conservancy of Arizona
Phoenix Zoo
Ronald McDonald House (Phoenix)
Salvation Army
Sierra Club
UNICEF

The Earth Cause Bell

The earth is Gaia, our mother. Her oceans, forests and resources need care and protection. The Earth Cause Bell was inspired by Earth Day 1990 and dedicated to the conservation of natural resources, support of recycling wherever possible and the preservation of our planet for future generations.

Photo by Jeffrey Manta, courtesy of the Cosanti Foundation

The Arcosanti buildings sit on top of a
mesa using only a small portion of the
acreage with the remainder of the property
left in a natural state.

The Workshops

For those willing to work at a variety of jobs, while living in camp-like conditions, Arcosanti offers workshops throughout the year. An intensive one-week seminar provides an in-depth look at the project along with environmental issues and Paolo Soleri's urban design philosophy. Four additional weeks offer participants a hands-on experience with silt casting, actual construction along with arcological philosophy.

Many American colleges and universities give academic credit for Arcosanti workshops. Fees are reasonable, $800 for the full five-week session covers the tuition along with room and board.

Through the Elderhostel program, people at least age 55 are encouraged to participate in Arcosanti workshops. Soleri particularly likes this group. "Elderhostel groups are most open to what we are talking about. It is fundamental to talk to young people but the Elderhostel participants have been through the experience. Many saw the materialistic affluence and believe something is going very badly," he reflects.

Numerous special programs are also offered throughout the year. Soleri's earth casting techniques for sculpture, windbells and architectural models are also taught.

A recent workshop on agriculture featured Californian Dave Blume, President of the International Institute for Ecological Agriculture, one of many organizations renting facilities at Arcosanti to put on their own program.

The new Paradox Internship Program which is under development at Arcosanti will explore the relationship of cyberspace and arcology. Although Soleri says, "I am most ignorant about cyberspace, I feel it is important to discuss what is going on."

Paolo Soleri, seated in back, meets with
new workshop participants to present the
philosophy of Arcosanti.

Francesca Ghelardoni, a philosophy student in Milan, Italy, felt closed into a lifestyle. She wanted to experience something new. After checking out the Arcosanti website, she came to Arizona. "It's wonderful, perfect – the wind, sun, silence, architecture. You turn the corner; there's something new. I think it's great that Paolo can do this."

Nicole Jardes, age 19, learned about Arcosanti through an organization called Interim. She decided to learn about construction and to experience an alternative living situation. Nicole was interested in the project as well as the sense of community: "I grew up in the country in New Hampshire, so I have enjoyed the interaction with people from several different cultures."

I got back yesterday and the shock was considerable. I haven't been back in England long, but already I've seen the news on the television and upon arrival seen the English people. I think of Arcosanti as an incredibly gentle place. There are always improvements to make and Arcosanti has many, but in comparison with the rest of the world, the majority of the people there are highly sensitive, intelligent, caring individuals and I am grateful to have met them. I found the inspirational people I was looking for and I will carry them with me now. I spent six months thinking about existence on this earth in a way very few people have a chance to do. Out in the real world we don't really know we're in a process of existence, the daily tasks and procedures make that impossible for most to achieve. But I had time thinking about everything before I thought about it, if that makes sense. A prelude to the thoughts which spawn action. Invaluable!"

James Rawlinson, from Surrey, England
on his Arcosanti experience.

Arcosanti Agriculture

Amanda Mehrer is the Agricultural Coordinator for Arcosanti. An Arizona native, her interest in the wilderness and desire to work directly with the land brought her to Arcosanti. "Here I can tap into opportunities to experiment and learn." Mehrer attended Hampshire College in Massachusetts where students design their own curriculum. "I concentrated on ecological restoration and landscape design."

Mehrer, who takes her inspiration from the Hopi Indians, says she draws a connection with the history of human habitation. "We plant native crops in the fertile flood plain. We work to minimize the impact on the land so, of course, growing organically fits into that. We are stewards of the land."

The planting of traditional gardens preserves water by using sunken beds for planting along with the use of mulch such as straw or leaves and sometimes newspapers. "Desert gardening is more challenging because of extreme temperature changes. We have to deal with hot days and sometimes cold temperatures at night along with wind and bugs," says Mehrer.

Since no fertilizer or chemical insecticides are used at Arcosanti, learning about the bug population is vital. Mehrer says, "We have to encourage the good predators such as beneficial insects who need pollen and nectar or insects such as ladybugs, spiders and the praying mantis who prey on aphids."

(continued)

Some herbal sprays with hot pepper and insecticide soap are used to control the bug population.

A surprising variety of crops are grown in the gardens and the field ranging from vegetables such as carrots, cucumbers, chard, okra, eggplant, tomatillos plus beans, squash and corn. In the orchard, there are peaches, and a small vineyard recently yielded enough grapes to bottle some wine.

During her off-time, Mehrer enjoys playing the guitar, painting and drawing but her most important goal is "really establishing an agriculture program here that can flourish. There is so much more that can be done."

(above)
Amanda Mehrer works in the greenhouse.

(facing page)
The yield from the peach trees allows for serving homemade peach ice cream during festival dinners.

Exploring Arcosanti

The Arcosanti acreage left natural offers splendid opportunities for viewing birds and animals. Birding enthusiasts will find hummingbirds, yellow finches, swallows, blue herons and the beautiful vermilion flycatcher. There are numerous birds of prey including owls, hawks and eagles, plus the scavenger turkey vultures.

As the terrain changes from Phoenix to the Arcosanti property, the striking saguaro cactus disappears. Here scrub oak, prickly pair, and mesquite along with cottonwood, juniper and acacia, natural to the landscape, take over. Arcosanti has added cypress, willows and olive trees from which the harvest yields bottled olives for sale in the Visitors' Gallery.

Among the many animals spotted on the Arcosanti property are herds of antelope, mountain lions, bobcats, skunks, javelina, and, on occasion, a brown bear has been spotted. There are numerous rabbits, quail, and roadrunners. Huge toads come out from their underground hiding places in the wet season. Scorpions and rattlesnakes are also a part of the scene. Pictured is the collared lizard.

From top left, clockwise:

- Desert lizard on Arcosanti hill
- Desert flower
- Barn at the Arcosanti ranch
- River in canyon east of Arcosanti

Pierre Teilhard de Chardin's Comments

Paolo Soleri frequently mentions Pierre Teilhard de Chardin, a French Jesuit whose writings reflect on Soleri's theological views. In his book *On Love and Happiness*, Teilhard de Chardin writes:

"... if we are to be happy – completely happy – we must in one way or another, directly or through some medium that gradually reaches out further afield (a line of research, a venture, an idea, perhaps or a cause), transfer the ultimate interest of our lives to the advancement and success of the world we live in."

In his book *The Heart of Matter*, Teilhard de Chardin states:

"Even in this century, men are still living as chance circumstances decide for them, with no aim but their daily bread or a quiet old age. You can count the few who fall under the spell of a task that far exceeds the dimensions of their individual lives...at this very moment, we are being given a glimpse of what a national effort can mean. Even so unless adult mankind is to drift aimlessly and so perish, it is essential that it rise to the concept of a specifically and integrally human effort. After having for so long done no more than allow itself to live, mankind will one day understand that the time has come to undertake its own development and to mark out its own road."

Influenced by the evolutionary philosophy of Teilhard de Chardin, Soleri believes with deep conviction that "we are not the children of divinity. We are the fathers of divinity. So it is our task to turn the physical universe into a divine universe."

Question to Paolo Soleri:
Is your idea to take the city as we know it today and bring it down to a smaller scale?

Response:
Yes, with a clear awareness that those things have to be set into some kind of a schedule that can be very long so the question is not to demolish what exists but to guide what we add to that which exists in ways which may be conducive finally to a new form more responsive to the needs of society and to the needs of the environment.

The Minds' Garden

In keeping with Soleri's emphasis on the natural environment, the Minds' Garden located near the town structures at the tip of the canyon, is set aside for residents and visitors alike to enjoy a moment of tranquillity. Here the undisturbed desert stretches out in front of the viewer who can catch a glimpse of the Agua Fria river plus desert creatures. Residents have left their mark with the occasional piece of sculpture that epitomizes the uniqueness of the Arcosanti staff and work participants. One such piece is the sculpture by Jan Zach located at the entry to Arcosanti. Seemingly made of metal, it is, in fact, sculpted out of marine plywood. The epoxy coating preserves its integrity and color.

The desert itself offers surprising diversity in what appears to be a hostile environment where temperatures can soar in the area surrounding Arcosanti to the low hundreds or drop as low as 30 degrees. A variety of organisms and plant life exist sometimes in a quiet dormant condition typical of the desert and dependent on the weather conditions and the time of day. But let it rain, then plants such as the grasses green up so quickly that what was seemingly brown and forever lost is now green and thriving. The smaller organisms come to life and inhabitants hidden previously appear in this new garden that seemed to be dead just hours before.

It's a place to reflect and imagine the smaller organisms that the naked-eye cannot observe such as microbes and bacteria. The symbiotic relationship between the lichen and algae, which grow on the rock structures, eventually cause the breakdown of the rock into soil. This process allows for larger plant growth on the hillside in unexpected places amidst the rock walls. All have a growth pattern in sync with the desert climate. Each of these organisms contributes an important part to the life cycle.

(above)
The Minds' Garden, located north of
Arcosanti.
(left)
Sculpture by Jan Zach.

Colly Soleri Music Center

Here is an ideal space for open-air concerts. The curved upper concrete panels with canvas stretched across the top to limit the sun give a natural appearance. The amphitheater seats 500.

The concert series began in 1980 in memory of Soleri's wife, Colly, who was very supportive of performing arts and cultural activities. Presented annually, concerts and light shows are held May through October. The series includes the Italian Night, Jazz Night, and the popular light and sound show, Pictograph 2000, in which the Arcosanti residents perform casting shadow figures on the face of the cliff.

The vaulted area, with its protection from the hot desert sun, also serves as a work area for the on-going construction project.

During summer, Italian Night at Arcosanti starts with a lively dinner that takes place in the open under the vaults. People come from all over Arizona and beyond to attend this popular event.

Paolo Soleri serves up the pasta from a wheelbarrow
during Italian Night.

Evening performance
in the Colly Soleri Music Center.

Earth Population

Aldo Leopold supports Soleri's theory about the need to preserve. In his book, *A Sand County Almanac*, Leopold stated that "humans are not a superior species with the right to manage and control the rest of nature, but rather humans are plain members of the biotic community. A thing is right when it tends to preserve the integrity, stability and beauty of the biotic community. It is wrong when it tends to do otherwise."

The following statistical data is worth considering when thinking about the effects of urban sprawl and the ongoing efforts of Paolo Soleri through his Arcosanti project:

• From the beginning of man to the 1800's, there was no city with a population of more than one million inhabitants.
• Two hundred years later, the population of 300 cities exceeds one million or more people.
• Today the world population is more than **six billion**.
• The **daily** growth of the world population is close to a quarter of a million. According to the Population Reference Bureau, 375,252 births occur every day.
• In a little more than a decade, more than one billion will be added to the world population. Almost half of that population increase will be in the United States since more than four million babies are born every year in the United States. The U.S. has one of the highest natural growth rates of any industrialized country in the world.
• By the year 2050, according to Negative Population Growth, Inc., the world population will be 9,309,051,539.
• The earth cannot support one or two billion with the lifestyle of middle class Americans.

Leopold's comments that "a thing is right when it tends to preserve the integrity, stability and beauty of the biotic community" and Soleri's dedication to preservation of the environment give cause for all humans to consider how we can best cope with the needs of humans and the needs of nature.

F rank Lloyd Wright built houses or buildings in harmony
with the environment that is why he was so famous.
*The problem is that we are deceiving ourselves because
one house in harmony with the environment is something
we can all agree on; but when you have to build two
billion houses, then you have a problem because they
are no longer in harmony with the environment. So there
is a delusional notion here, and it is the delusion that is
destroying us.*

*So my idea is to build the opposite because I believe
that's the way of the living world. Any lean system is not
an explosion of things but an implosion of things, a coming
together of things. We are not even beginning to accept
this notion, really, of life being totally dependent on the
coming together of things.*

Paolo Soleri

Quote from Book, *Ecological Design*

In their book *Ecological Design*, Sim van der Ryn and Stuart Cowan, offer the following view of sustainability:

> The word sustainability has become a kind of mantra for the 1990s, offering the possibility of balance and permanence in a world where we experience precisely the opposite. Today, our rapid exploitation of fossil fuels is already changing climate patterns so catastrophically that many insurance companies will no longer insure against extreme weather events. One hundred square miles of rainforest are being lost each day. Species are going extinct at the unprecedented rate of three per hour. Chemicals once thought relatively harmless to humans are turning out to affect immune and endocrine systems. The list of environmental damage is endless, from the depleted soils of the cornbelt to the vast industrial disaster zones of Eastern Europe and the former Soviet Union. In search of comfort, convenience, and material wealth, we have begun to sacrifice not only our own health, but also the health of all species. We are starting to exhaust the capacity of the very systems that sustain us, and now we must deal with the consequences.
>
> Ecological sustainability, in contrast, is the task of finding alternatives to the practices that got us into trouble in the first place; it is necessary to rethink agriculture, shelter, energy use, urban design, transportation, economics, community patterns, resource use, forestry, the importance of wilderness, and our central values.
>
> There are strip malls, mini-malls, regional malls, industrial parks, edge cities, detached single-family homes, townhouses, and sealed high-rises, all hooked up with an environmentally devastating infrastructure of roads, highways, storm and sanitary sewers, power lines, and the rest. The pattern of these templates has become the pattern of our everyday experience, insinuating itself into our own awareness of place and nature.
>
> City planners, engineers, and other design professionals have gotten trapped in standardized solutions that require enormous expenditures of energy and resources to implement. These standard templates, available as off the shelf recipes, are unconsciously adopted and replicated on a vast scale. The result might be called dumb design: design that fails to consider the health of human communities or of ecosystems, let alone the prerequisites of creating an actual place.

Van der Ryn and Cowan speak of finding alternatives to the practices that have caused the depletion of resources. Paolo Soleri seeks to find answers through the on-going laboratory work in progress at Arcosanti.

Need to Conserve

The burning of fossil fuels, such as coal, oil and gas, adds 6 billion metric tons of carbon to the atmosphere each year. The Executive Director of Ozone Action, John Passacantando, writes in the 1996 Annual Report, "The U.S. has been responsible for 30 percent of the total production of ozone depleting chemicals and contributes nearly a quarter of the global carbon dioxide emissions. The adoption of environmentally sound practices is therefore necessary not only in the developing world, which is struggling to improve its industry and agriculture, but also in advanced countries."

The use of toxic chemicals and fossil fuels, together with the burning and logging of forests which reduces carbon storage by trees, causes upheaval in the climate, irreparable damage to eco-systems, changes in crop yields, health problems and even death due to severe weather changes causing droughts, flooding and heat waves.

Soleri emphatically advocates that miniaturization provides answers "by reducing the needs of the individual, the impact on the environment is reduced thereby allowing for harmony through a more complex approach." His approach further allows for human beings to thrive "in a higher and more spirited context."

The challenges are clear. Our generation must work to conserve and to minimize adverse impacts. We can learn through programs such as Arcosanti to make better choices every day by reducing materialistic needs. Soleri addresses these concerns but the success depends on all of us.

Visitors in the foundry are focused on the bell making process.

Tours of Arcosanti offer in-depth information on Soleri's futuristic environments that may some day be found even on the oceans and in outer space. Conversant tour guides, such as Joe Henson lead visitors to viewing points where they can gain a better understanding of life in Soleri's arcologies. Henson accepts a deeply felt responsibility to educate people about how this concept could work in every city in the world. "One of the thrills I get out of life is passing this information on," he explains.

Henson also manages the Visitors' Gallery operation where hundreds of Arcosanti bells are found along with a variety of Arcosanti remembrances, including books and the Soleri video on Arcosanti. Each year, two Arcosanti residents' works are featured in the Gallery. In 1998, the beaded jewelry of Bakery Manager, Linda Fournier, and the metal sculptures of Ron Chandler, the Maintenance Coordinator, were selected. Chandler's electronic bugs satirize the computer industry. Fournier, who has been at Arcosanti for 9 years, uses natural forms and colors in her jewelry. "I like the natural forms such as ceramic, bone, horn and shells to create more texture with the glass beads. The desert colors here affect my work too and are reflected in the choices of beads. I use pale greens, turquoise, browns and pinks and purples seen in the sunsets."

A variety of Arcosanti grown preserves, olives and sage sticks are also available for purchase in the Visitors' Gallery.

Although frugal, the Arcosanti guest rooms offer reasonable prices along with impressive desert views. The setting, with a minimum of city lights, allows for exquisite star gazing. Elderhostel participants are accommodated in the Greenhouse guest rooms where some bathrooms are shared, indicative of the economy of the project. The *sky suite*, pictured here, has two bedrooms with a kitchenette. Perched high up in the project, views from these rooms are also breathtaking.

HOW YOU CAN HELP

The kinds of things you can do to help insure the future of Arcosanti are:

• **Visit Arcosanti and Cosanti**. Take your friends and family there. Your donations for the guided walking tour of Arcosanti or the self-guided tour of Cosanti are an important part of the Foundation's income.

• **Purchase ceramic and bronze wind-bells**, assemblies and sculptures designed and made by Paolo Soleri sold at both Cosanti and Arcosanti. Proceeds support the construction at Arcosanti and the Foundation's educational programs. Overnight accommodations are available at Arcosanti by reservation.

• **Plan a day or event** at Arcosanti or Cosanti for your group. The Foundation's staff is eager to work with groups to develop special day-programs which can include tours, lunch or snacks, foundry or silt casting tours, nature walks, or slide shows. Meeting space and overnight accommodations by reservation are available for your event or retreat.

• **Participate in one of the Cosanti Foundation's educational programs.** Learn more about Arcosanti and Paolo Soleri's work by participating in the one-week Arcosanti workshop seminar or jump right in and help build Arcosanti yourself by participating in the full five-week workshop, which includes four weeks of construction, maintenance work and participation in all aspects of daily life at Arcosanti. The one-week siltcasting workshop gives participants experience with the wash-away silt and earth casting techniques developed by Paolo Soleri. For those 55 and over a range of one-week programs are available through the Elderhostel program at Arcosanti.

• Ask to be placed on the Cosanti Foundation Special Events mailing list and attend the wide range of seminars, lectures and concerts at Arcosanti.

Or, you can consider a variety of ways to donate goods or services:

Make a tax deductible donation to the Cosanti Foundation. Monetary donations are important to the continued construction of Arcosanti. You or your business can also help by making in-kind donations of the products used to build and outfit Arcosanti. The Foundation's staff can help coordinate donations of construction materials, tools, vehicles, office furnishings, computer products, office supplies, appliances or furnishings, alternative energy production equipment, landscaping or gardening supplies.

Or maybe you have a talent you can share. A wide range of professional services is needed by the Foundation each year. Donate your professional skills so the cost of such services can go into construction or educational programming.

You can specify which program or project at Arcosanti you would like your donation to benefit. Or you can underwrite an entire project or program. Current and ongoing projects include:

• Paving the road to Arcosanti.

• Construction of a wide variety of facilities in the East Crescent, an award winning multi-use neighborhood surrounding the Colly Soleri Amphitheater now under construction.

• Maintenance and expansion of the Paolo Soleri archives at Arcosanti and building facilities in the East Crescent to house and display this important collection.

• Continued development of the agriculture program at Arcosanti.

• Maintenance and restoration of Cosanti, an Arizona Historic Site.

• Development of the Foundation's programs using digital technology such as its website, computer graphics, the virtual Arcosanti model and educational programming in this realm.

• Development of and landscaping around the pond to create a year-round recreational asset.

• Continued restoration of the riparian habitat to diminish the effects of cattle ranching in the area.

• Scholarships for students to participate in the Arcosanti Workshop program or internships for students who wish to spend more than five weeks working at Arcosanti.

For more information, contact:

Arcosanti
HC 74, Box 4136
Mayer AZ 86333
Phone: (520) 632-7135

Cosanti
6433 Doubletree Ranch Road
Scottsdale AZ 85253
Phone: (480) 948-6145

Website: http://www.arcosanti.org/

Soleri's futuristic models adorn the walls of the Visitors' Gallery and are also found in the restaurant. A copy of Soleri's book, *Arcology: City in the Image of Man*, published by MIT Press in 1970 and now out of print, is also available in the Visitors' Gallery for anyone interested in studying his plans for cities that would float, could be suspended over a canyon, or launched in outer space.

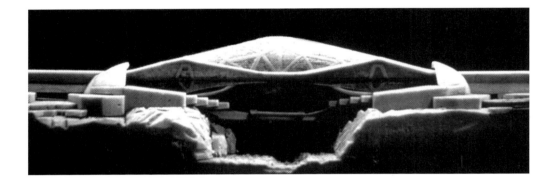

Stonebow

A bridge stretching from one side of an abyss to the other. Up to 200,000 people, on just over 300 acres, would live suspended above a ravine or deep canyon. Residents would have choices of various climactic conditions along with awesome views of nature and varied botanical specimens. Soleri says, "To remind man of the miracle of life emerging and perpetuating itself in endless ways is not a fringe benefit for urban man. It is one of the cultural aspects of a truly civilized condition."

Asteromo

This city would hover in outer space with a population of 30,000. "Miniaturization is the password to the fantastic voyage," says Soleri. Asteromo is basically a double-skinned cylinder kept inflated by pressurization and rotation on its main axis. It is lined with vegetation for food and the carbon-dioxide cycle. This is a research based space community.

Bibliography

Brown, Jerry. *Dialogues*. Berkeley Hills Books, 1998.

Teilhard de Chardin, Pierre. *On Love and Happiness*.
    Harper & Row, San Francisco, CA, 1984.

Teilhard de Chardin, Pierre. *The Heart of the Matter*.
    translated by Rene Hague, Harcourt Brace & Co, 1991.

Leopold, Aldo. *A Sand County Almanac*.
    Oxford University Press, New York, 1948

Soleri, Paolo. *Arcosanti, An Urban Laboratory?*
    The Cosanti Press, Scottsdale, AZ, 1993.

Soleri, Paolo. *Arcology: The City in the Image of Man*.
    MIT Press, Cambridge, MA, 1969.

Soleri, Paolo. *The Omega Seed: An Eschatological Hypothesis*.
    Anchor Press/Doubleday, Garden City, NY, 1981.

Soleri's Cities: Architecture for Planet Earth and Beyond.
    Video by Home Vision

Van der Ryn, Sim and Cowan, Stuart. *Ecological Design*.
    Island Press, Washington D.C. / Covelo CA, 1996.

Index

Timelines

1919	Paolo Soleri born in Torino, Italy.
1933	Moved with family to Grenoble, France; attended Ecole d'Art Industriel.
1935-39	Continued education at Torino Academia Albertine in Italy.
1941-46	Studied at Torino Polytechnico; graduated with a Ph.D. in architecture.
1947-48	Came to the U. S. as a Fellow of the Frank Lloyd Wright Foundation.
1949	Collaborated with Mark Mills in designing Dome House in Cave Creek, Arizona.
1949	Married Colly Wood.
1950-55	Returned to Italy. Submitted proposal, Cosmic Potentials, to MIT.
1951-52	Designed and built a ceramics factory in Vietri Sul Mare, Italy.
1956	Settled in Scottsdale with his wife, Colly, and two daughters. Purchased land that became the Cosanti Foundation.
1962	Cosanti Foundation founded to serve as organization through which Soleri's philosophical, educational, research and construction work is performed.
1963	Awarded American Institute of Architects Gold Medal for Craftsmanship.
1969	Publication of Arcology research in the book: *Arcology, The City in the Image of Man*, (MIT Press).
1970	Ground broken at Arcosanti.
1970	Architectural Vision exhibit at the Corcoran Gallery in Washington D.C. and at several large museums in the U.S. and Canada.

1971	Commissioned by the Phoenix Civic Center Management Board to design a sculpture, *Il Donnone*, which was installed at the Phoenix Art Museum.
1973	Publication of *The Bridge Between Matter and Spirit is Matter Becoming Spirit*, (Doubleday).
1976	Major exhibition, *Two Suns Arcology, The City Energized by the Sun*, at Xerox Square, Rochester NY.
1979	Received Progressive Architecture magazine architectural design citation for East Crescent complex.
1981	Designed and constructed DeConcini House in Phoenix, Arizona.
1989	Presented with the Utopus Award by the Third International Conference of Utopian Studies at the Universita Degli Studi di Genova in Reggio Calabria, Italy.
1994	Asteromo '94 model commissioned and built for the Mei Center for the Arts in Japan.
1995	Commissioned to design and build amphitheater at Glendale Community College, Glendale Arizona.
1996	Commissioned to design pedestrian bridges for the Scottsdale AZ canal project.
1996	Commissioned by the Japanese Hyper Building Research Committee to design and display Hyper Building Arcology at a Symposium in Tokyo.

**See website: www.Arcosanti.org
for additional information.**

Definition of words used by Paolo Soleri:

Arcology
A combination of the words architecture and ecology. Arcology is Paolo Soleri's concept of cities that embody the fusion of architecture and ecology working as one integral process to produce new urban habitats.

Arcologies
To blend architecture and ecology in the production of new urban environments encompassing all aspects of life including cultural, residential and commercial.

Arcosanti
The word derives from Arcology and Cosanti meaning architecture and ecology in harmony with the environment. The Arcosanti project represents a renaissance of thinking about how we build cities. The purpose is to investigate and experiment with arcological concepts. To integrate living, learning and working is one of the main goals of the project. The three-dimensional city because of its true efficiency is also respectful of the earth's ecological systems and its atmosphere. It does not pollute the earth.

Cosanti
From the Italian words *cosa*, meaning thing and *anti*, meaning before or against, which expresses a philosophy of anti-materialism. Cosanti is a term created by Paolo Soleri to express the basis of his life's work. Cosanti houses the Scottsdale offices of the Cosanti Foundation and is also the headquarters for the Cosanti Originals bells on display in Scottsdale and in the Visitors' Gallery at Arcosanti.

Miniaturization
To maximize benefits of urban life but to minimize the use of land, raw materials and energy.

Postscript

I would like to think that I will be remembered for nudging reality a tiny infinitesimal step toward self-revelation. That means that all of the evolutionary processes turn out eventually to be the best effort, the only effort that reality is putting up to become knowledgeable of itself. I feel that is self-revelation—a great quest for reality to get to know itself.

Urban sprawl causes both segregation and isolation. A miniaturized town such as Arcosanti brings back a sense of community.

Coming together is where life gets its own reality.

Paolo Soleri